ELEPHANTS

By Sophie Lockwood

Content Adviser: Barbara E. Brown, Scientific Associate, Mammal Division, Field Museum of Chicago

THE CHILD'S WORLD®, MANKATO, MINNESOTA

Elephants

Published in the United States of America by The Child's World®
1980 Lookout Drive • Mankato, MN 56003-1705
800-599-READ • www.childsworld.com

Acknowledgements:

The Child's World®: Mary Berendes, Publishing Director

The Creative Spark: Mary Francis, Project Director; Wendy Mead, Editor; Deborah Goodsite, Photo Researcher

The Design Lab: Kathleen Petelinsek, Designer and Production Artist

Photos:

Cover: Alexey Stiop/iStockphoto.com; frontispiece and page 4: Mark Atkins/iStockphoto.com; half title: Hedda Gjerpen/iStockphoto.com.

Interior: Alamy: 26 (Ross Warner), 5 bottom left and 34–35 (Neil McAllister); Animals Animals: 10 (Peter Weimann); AP Photo: 36 (Jon Hrusa/IFAW); Getty: 5 top left and 9 (Michael Nichols/National Geographic), 5 bottom right and 25 (Frank Zeller/AFP), 32 (Alexander Joe/AFP); iStockphoto.com: 5 top right and 12 (Eromaze/iStockphoto.com), 16–17 (Davidjk05/iStockphoto.com); Jupiterimages: 5 center left and 22 (Martyn Colbeck/Oxford Scientific); Ron Kimball Stock Photography: 29 (Tom and Pat Leeson); Minden Pictures: 30 (Chris Newbert); Peter Arnold Inc.: 19 (Michel & Christine Denis-Huot/Auteurs/BIOS); Photolibrary Group: 20–21; SuperStock: 15 (age fotostock).

Library of Congress Cataloging-in-Publication Data

Lockwood, Sophie.
  Elephants / by Sophie Lockwood.
    p. cm. — (The world of mammals)
  Includes index.
  ISBN 978-1-59296-928-9 (library bound : alk. paper)
  1. Elephants—Juvenile literature. I. Title. II. Series.
  QL737.P98L63 2008
  599.67—dc22   2007021942

TABLE OF CONTENTS

chapter one | **MOTHERS RULE** | 6

chapter two | **FROM TRUNK TO TAIL** | 11

chapter three | **PATTERNS OF LIFE** | 16

chapter four | **ELEPHANTS ON PARADE** | 24

chapter five | **THE PAST, PRESENT, AND FUTURE** | 31

Glossary, 38
For More Information, 39
The Animal Kingdom—Where Do Elephants Fit In?, 39
Index, 40

Chapter One

Mothers Rule

In Zakouma National Park in Africa, an elderly female elephant browses on acacia leaves. Her trunk is so agile that she can pick single leaves from the tree branches. The cow elephant is fifty-six years old, and her eyes show the wisdom of every drought, every storm, and every flood in her long life. She knows where to find food when **forage** is scarce and where to find water when the rains do not come. African elephants eat up to twenty hours a day, so good forage—plant food the elephants eat—is important. The female is the **matriarch,** the leader of the herd.

Zakouma covers 3,108 square kilometers (1,200 square miles) of southeastern Chad. In the past twenty years, its elephant population has grown from 1,100 to 3,500. This growth is both a blessing and a burden. Zakouma provides a safe haven for elephants, buffalo, hartebeests, waterbuck, topi, reedbuck, and giraffes. However, these animals are **herbivores,** and an area as small as Zakouma struggles to feed so many.

Did You Know?
Forest elephants (*Loxodonta cyclotis*) eat 100 to 300 kilograms (220 to 660 pounds) of grass, shrubs, bark, and leaves each day. They drink about 190 liters (50 gallons) of water daily.

The map on the right shows the range of the African elephant.

The matriarch is a forest elephant, one of two elephant species that live in Africa. She stands 2.7 meters (9 feet) tall at the shoulder, measures nearly 7 meters (23 feet) long, and weighs 3 metric tons (3.3 tons). Forest elephants are smaller than their savanna cousins and have been called pygmy elephants. It is hard to imagine that an animal so large could be a "pygmy" anything.

As the rainy season begins, the matriarch heads beyond the park's borders in search of fresh forage. An elephant herd always follows the matriarch. They are her daughters, granddaughters, great-granddaughters, and young male relatives. As they move northward, more and more elephants follow the matriarch's lead. Soon, the herd numbers nearly one thousand animals.

The first major stop on the five-month journey the elephants will undertake is Andouma water hole. The elephants walk into the water and drink. Then they fill their trunks and spray water over their backs, like a self-controlled shower. At the edge of the water hole, elephant calves wallow in the mud. They roll over and over, coating themselves so heavily that they look red-orange rather than gray. Some of the herd submerge themselves, using their trunks like snorkels.

Did You Know?
African elephants begin growing tusks at around eighteen months to two years old. Forest elephants have straight tusks with a pinkish tinge, while their savanna cousins have longer, curved tusks that can be slightly yellow in color.

Once the elephants leave the park, they are in danger. Poachers know the routes elephants travel and do not think twice about killing elephants for their tusks. The material tusks are made of is also known as **ivory.** Even though the sale of ivory has been banned since 1989, there are still places to sell illegal ivory, called black markets. Although the sale was illegal, 1 kilogram (2.2 pounds) of high-quality ivory sold for $200 in 2004. By 2006, ivory sold for $750 per kilogram. An average tusk on a full-grown sixty-year-old elephant weighs about 61 kilograms (135 pounds). Buyers of poached ivory can be found in China, Japan, and other Asian and Middle Eastern nations. Purchasers turn the

A large herd of African elephants looks for food inside Zakouma National Park.

ivory into signature stamps, statuettes, knife handles, and chopsticks. Most of these products are sold in the Middle East and Asia.

By October, the elephants of Zakouma return to the park. The herd that numbered one thousand last March has lost seventy-five adult animals. A handful of these deaths were caused by old age, illness, and accidents. The rest come from the elephants' most dangerous **predators**—humans with rifles. The carcasses of elephants robbed of their ivory lay rotting on the ground. Their flesh feeds the vultures, hyenas, and golden jackals living outside Zakouma's borders.

Would You Believe?
Adult male forest elephants grow twice as large as females. A full-grown adult male weighs 6 metric tons (6.6 tons), compared to a female's 3 metric tons (3.3 tons). Males on the savanna are also more than twice the size of females—up to 7.7 metric tons (8.5 tons) compared to 2.7 metric tons (3 tons).

Elephants, such as these forest elephants, are sometimes killed for their tusks, or ivory.

Chapter Two

From Trunk to Tail

Elephants fascinate humans because of their size, tusks, trunks, ears, and skin. Adult African elephants (*Loxodonta africana*) are twice as tall as the average human. Full-size males weigh 6 metric tons (6.6 tons) or more, a weight equal to a large pickup truck. Tusks can measure just over 2 meters (6.6 feet). The elephants' entire bodies—including tusks—grow throughout their lives. Not only the largest land animals, elephants have also remarkably long lives. An elephant can live for about seventy years.

One of the most agile, flexible, and useful parts of the elephant is the trunk. Baby elephants must learn how to use their trunks. A one-year-old elephant calf tries repeatedly to suck in water and spray it out of its trunk. The calf sees the adults around it do this every day at the water hole. The calf tries and fails. Using a trunk takes practice. Discouraged, the calf lies down on its side and sucks its trunk, just like a two-year-old human child sucks his or her thumb.

Did You Know?
There are no bones in an elephant's trunk. It consists of about 150,000 individual muscles and nerves. These muscles give the trunk remarkable flexibility. Elephants use their trunks to spray water, scratch tired eyes, and pick up food—from grasses to a tiny peanut.

African elephants have two tips—like fingers—on their trunks, while Asian elephants (*Elephas maximus*) have only one tip. A trunk is strong enough to lift a tree trunk and sensitive enough to pick up a nickel. Elephants breathe through their trunks, but they also use their trunks like hands to put

An Asian elephant uses its trunk to toss dirt onto its back.

food into their mouths. They can suck up water and spray it into their mouths or over their backs. After a shower, an elephant uses its trunk to take up dust and soil and sprays it over its body. This provides a dusting of soil that protects the elephant's skin from sunburn and insects.

Did You Know?
Elephants, unlike other mammals, must keep at least one foot on the ground at all times. They cannot leap, gallop, or trot. An elephant walks at a rate of 6 kilometers per hour (4 miles per hour). When in a hurry, elephants move along at 25 kilometers per hour (16 miles per hour).

The skin on an elephant can measure 2.5 centimeters (1 inch) thick on the head, back, and the soles of the feet. Like human skin, elephant skin is sensitive to touch. Like other mammals, elephants have hair on their skin. The hair is coarse, bristly, and rather sparse. Adults investigate strange objects or wake sleeping infants with the tender skin of their hind feet. They can feel insect bites and scratch their bodies on rocks or tree trunks to ease the itch.

Although thick on most of the body, elephant skin is paper-thin on the insides of the ears and around the mouth. Ears perform several important jobs for elephants. When an elephant gets overheated, flapping the ears reduces that heat. Flapping the ears can also signal excitement or show an outward threat.

Because elephants are so large, they have few predators. A pride of lions may attack a baby elephant found on its own but would rarely attack an adult. In the Tsavo region of Kenya, lions do attack adults, but the elephants get excellent protection from their thick hides, powerful trunks, and tusks. Elephants have been also known to trample their attackers under their feet.

Tusks are two of an elephant's many teeth. Elephants have twelve **incisors** for cutting and twelve molars for grinding food. Infants are born with teeth and develop new, larger teeth as they grow. Tusks are overgrown incisors. Because elephants are forever chewing, their teeth wear down. As with human children, elephants lose their teeth and new ones move into the empty spaces. Unlike humans, elephants get six sets of teeth during their lives. The first set is replaced at about two or three years old. Tusks are also a great place to hang a 136-kilogram (300-pound) trunk to give it a rest.

Elephant tusks begin to emerge at eighteen months for males and two years for females. Tusks grow continuously

throughout an elephant's life. The average growth rate of tusks is 17 centimeters (6.7 inches) per year.

The killing of elephants for ivory has brought about changes in African elephants. As the largest bulls with the longest tusks were killed, females began mating with shorter-tusked males. Today, some elephants do not grow tusks at all or grow shorter, less desirable tusks. Oddly, this may be the thing that will save elephants. If there is no ivory, there is no reason to kill the elephants.

This baby African elephant won't grow tusks for another year.

Would You Believe?
The longest tusks on record measured 3.26 meters (10.7 feet). Only two-thirds of a tusk is visible. The other third is set into the elephant's skull.

Chapter Three

Patterns of Life

Adult savanna elephants need plenty of food. While elephants prefer grass and tender leaves, they will also eat fruits, roots, herbs, and small branches. As farms crowd elephants into smaller territories, hungry bulls and cows head to fields to dine on farm crops.

To prevent elephants from stealing human food growing in fields, scientists ran an interesting experiment, supported by the Elephant Pepper Development Trust. Farmers were encouraged to grow chili peppers around the perimeter of their crop fields. Since 1997, growing chili peppers has reduced elephants' crop raiding and provided farmers with an added cash crop.

Elephants learn to avoid fields with chili peppers because they are intelligent animals. Elephant brains are small compared to their massive bodies, but the brains still weigh 4 to 6 kilograms (8.8 to 13.2 pounds). The saying "An elephant never forgets" is not

Would You Believe?
Asian elephants have a sweet tooth. In addition to normal grasses and leaves, they also like bananas, mangoes, apples, coconuts, and sugarcane.

*These African elephants are approaching a water hole
where they can get a drink or take a bath.*

true, but it is not far off. Elephants learn routes to food and water sources. They recognize friends and family. If they are present at the death of a family member, they remember the site where the death took place. Some scientists believe that elephants mourn the deaths of friends and relatives.

Another sign of intelligence is that elephants have learned how to use tools. An elephant with an itch will use a small branch held in its trunk as a back scratcher. Leafy branches work well as flyswatters. Stones make excellent weapons to toss at an annoying animal. Toenails, trunks, and tusks working together can dig up tasty roots.

KEYSTONE SPECIES

Elephants are a **keystone species** of the forest, the savanna, and the Asian jungles. A keystone species is one that other species rely on for survival. Such a species can change its environment. Elephants knock down trees that invade the savanna, making way for healthy grass to grow. During drought, elephants know how to find water, and they dig water holes that provide drinks for other species. As they feed, elephants

consume seeds from grasses, flowers, and fruit. When they pass dung, they may be miles away from where they ate. That dung carries seeds, spreads fertilizer, and introduces plants to new locations.

Both plant and animal life change when elephants disappear from the savanna. Trees take over the grasslands, bringing with them birds, monkeys, and other tree-dwelling critters. Grazers that need sprawling, open plains—zebras, wildebeests, and buffaloes—depart. The largest grazers that remain are antelope, and they are far too small and swift to be quality prey for hungry lions. Hyenas, jackals, vultures, and other animals that feed on the lions' leftovers have to

This young African elephant is using a branch to scratch an itch.

hunt for themselves. Even the scarab beetles that survive by laying eggs in elephant dung will need to find a new home.

SOCIAL ANIMALS

Elephants have distinct social patterns. The females and their young follow one pattern, and the males follow another. A matriarch leads a herd of related females. Females stay with the herd throughout their lives. Males leave when they reach **puberty,** at about twelve to fourteen years old. A family herd or unit has from six to seventy elephants. On occasion, several units meet up and form a clan called a superherd, such as the **migrating** herds of Zakouma.

The matriarch decides when and where the herd eats and drinks. She knows where to find water and fresh grasses. All elephants need quantities of salt, and the matriarch leads the herd to salt licks, or places with naturally occurring salt. In Kitum Cave, on Mount Elgon in Kenya, elephants make their way through the dark to their personal salt lick. They mine the salt from the cave walls and ceilings.

A female has mated and become pregnant. She carries her calf for about twenty-two months. When the calf is born, the matriarch helps the mother. At birth, the baby weighs between 80 and 113 kilograms (175 and 250

This Asian elephant is digging for salt, an important part of the animal's diet.

pounds) and stands about 0.95 meters (3.1 feet) tall. The calf stands up and walks almost immediately and hurries to its mother's nipple. The nipples are located just behind the front legs. Baby elephants drink with their mouths, not their trunks. Infants grow quickly, gaining about 1 kilogram (2.2 pounds) a day if they nurse regularly. Female African elephants nurse each other's calves. If danger comes near, the matriarch rallies the other adults to circle the infants and protect them.

Juvenile elephants prepare for their roles in later life. Young cows become babysitters of the infants in the

Two juvenile male African elephants play fight.

herd. They learn parenting skills from their mothers, sisters, and aunts. Young bulls get ready for a life among bigger, stronger males. As juveniles, they practice sparring. Later in life, successful sparring will lead to being granted mating rights with females.

At twelve years old, males are less than half the size they will be when fully grown. Over the next two years, they must leave their family units to join bachelor herds. Males become sexually mature at about seventeen years old. They enter periods of sexual readiness called **musth.** Young males can go a bit wild during musth, and older males teach the young ones how to control their aggression.

In normal elephant societies, the young learn from birth how to behave as proper elephants. Matriarchs and older females discipline young elephants, and bulls control bachelor males when they are older. Without the benefit of herd life, elephants can go wild. In South Africa, many orphaned male elephants were raised without a herd influence, as elders were culled to control the elephant population in a national park. Without adult discipline, these young males grew aggressive, attacking and killing thirty-six endangered rhinos. To get the adolescent males under control, rangers brought in six mature bulls. The killings stopped because the older males taught the young males proper manners.

Chapter Four

Elephants on Parade

In the village of Hongsa, Laos, in southeastern Asia, residents prepare for the annual elephant festival. For the thirty thousand Laotians living in the district, the elephant is sacred. Laos is called "Land of a Million Elephants," although that number is far from accurate. The country has only two thousand wild and eight hundred working elephants. For centuries, elephants and Laotians have shared a close relationship. Expert trainers called **mahouts** held a place of honor in local villages. Today, the status that went with being a mahout has disappeared—along with thousands of native elephants.

Elephants are found only in Africa and Asia. Savanna or bush elephants and forest elephants are the two African species of elephants. There are four **subspecies** of Asian elephants. They are the Indian, Sumatran, Sri Lankan, and Borneo elephants.

All elephants share a number of common characteristics. They must have water and food daily. They are all

plant eaters, grazing on grasses, reeds, leaves, and shrubs. Elephants have an excellent sense of smell and live in groups called herds. Elephants must migrate throughout the year, looking for water and fresh food.

AFRICAN ELEPHANTS

Savanna or bush elephants are, by far, the largest species of elephants. Their most recognizable features are large ears shaped like the continent of Africa and long, curving tusks. Savanna elephants live in open woodland and on grassy plains. They can be found on

A male Asian elephant marches in a parade during a Laotian elephant festival.

Did You Know?
Elephants have toenails. African elephants have five toenails on their front feet and three toenails on their hind feet. Asian elephants have five toenails on their front feet and four toenails on their hind feet.

the eastern and southern plains of Africa. Thanks to legal protection and careful monitoring, the savanna elephant population in southern Africa is growing. Up to 300,000 elephants roam the region.

Forest elephants are smaller and darker skinned than their savanna cousins. Scientists measure populations of forest elephants by the hundreds rather than the thousands. Forest elephants have straighter tusks and rounder ears. They live in dense jungles in small, female-run herds. Poaching takes its toll on forest elephant herds. It is easier to kill these elephants and escape capture than it is to kill elephants and escape on open savannas.

Would You Believe?
The largest known specimen of African elephant weighed 10 metric tons (22,000 pounds).

This African elephant is scratching himself on some rough tree bark in Tanzania.

ASIAN ELEPHANTS

The most common Asian elephant is the Indian elephant. Although this subspecies is named for the country of India, these elephants are also found in Bangladesh, Bhutan, Brunei, Cambodia, China, Laos, Malaysia, Nepal, Thailand, and Vietnam. Indian elephants are shorter and weigh less than African elephants. An adult bull weighs, on average, 3,182 to 5,000 kilograms (7,000 to 11,000 pounds) and stands 3.3 meters (10.8 feet) at the shoulder.

It is easy to identify an Indian elephant. The skin is dark gray, and the ears are rounder and smaller than those of an African elephant. The trunk has only one "finger," and the forehead has two very noticeable bumps. Males have ivory tusks, but the females either have no tusks or very short ones.

Sumatran elephants are small, measuring 1.7 to 2.6 meters (5.6 to 8.5 feet) at the shoulder. Fewer than 3,500 Sumatran elephants exist in the wild. They live on the island of Sumatra, and the population suffers from loss of habitat. Sumatran elephants feed on leaves, vines, bananas, ginger, and tender bamboo shoots.

Sri Lankan elephants are particularly important to their island nation. They are protected under the Sri Lanka Fauna

and Flora Protection Ordinance, and being convicted of killing an elephant leads to a death sentence. Sri Lanka elephants are dark gray—almost black—with patches of pink skin on the ears, face, trunk, and belly. These elephants frequently come into conflict with humans because they like eating such farm crops as bananas, sugarcane, and other cultivated fruits. The population count stands between 3,200 and 4,400 elephants.

Recently, scientists have determined that elephants on the island of Borneo are a separate subspecies. Borneo elephants are the smallest elephants. Males reach a maximum of 2.5 meters (8.2 feet) at the shoulder. Borneo elephants are chubby through the body, with baby-elephant faces and long tails that reach nearly to the ground. Only about one thousand Borneo elephants live in the world.

STRANGE RELATIONS

Elephants have a number of close relatives, although most people could not possibly guess what those relatives are. One relative is the dugong, a marine mammal that is found in Africa, Asia, and Australia. Another related species is the manatee, a marine mammal that lives in parts of Asia, Africa, the West Indies, and North and South America—commonly called sea cows.

An Asian elephant calls out to other members of its herd.

Hyraxes are also distant cousins of elephants. These tiny rodents are furry, round critters with short, stumpy tails. They seem unlike elephants in every possible way, yet scientists can trace a clear relationship between these 2-kilogram (4.4-pound) fuzzy creatures and 7,000-kilogram (15,400-pound) elephants.

The manatee is a close relative of the elephant.

Chapter Five

The Past, Present, and Future

Sometime between 45 and 55 million years ago, the first ancestors of elephants roamed the earth. Those first elephants—*Moeritherium*—looked nothing like the elephants of today. They looked more like hippos or tapirs and were the size of a large pig. They stood about 60 centimeters (2 feet) at the shoulder and had no trunk or tusks.

It took millions of years for *Moeritherium* to become anything vaguely like an elephant. Through fossils, scientists have uncovered more than 150 different elephant species, including the Ice Age woolly mammoths and mastodons. By the time those species came around, early elephants had developed huge bodies, long trunks, and serious tusks.

Today, between 400,000 and 660,000 elephants live in Africa. In the far south, elephants not only thrive, their populations are growing. In East Africa, great herds

challenge growing human populations
for land. In the forests of western Africa,
poachers endanger elephant survival. Along

An African elephant crosses a busy road in Zambia.

the edge of the Sahara and in the Namib Desert, a few elephant herds thrive despite the dry desert climate, trekking over burning sands to find water.

THREATS TO SURVIVAL

In the 1930s and 1940s, as many as three to five million elephants browsed in the grasslands and lowland jungles of Africa. Then, humans began hunting elephants as trophies and for ivory. During the 1980s, humans killed an estimated 100,000 elephants each year. In some areas, four out of five elephants in every herd died to satisfy human greed.

In Asia, elephants are seriously endangered because human populations turn elephant habitats into farms. In India, elephants kill two hundred people each year, and one hundred elephants die as humans take their revenge. With elephant populations so small to begin with, the slaying of one hundred elephants a year is a devastating loss.

Even working elephants are in danger. Humans have tamed and worked Asian elephants for more than four thousand years. Most of these elephants work in the timber industry. They lift and carry large logs through dense forests. As nations put bans on logging, elephants and their mahouts find themselves out of work. Most elephant owners cannot afford to keep a non-working elephant, but these animals cannot return to the wild. They do not know how to live as wild elephants. Only in Myanmar, where extensive logging continues, are elephants' jobs safe for at least the next ten years. In other Asian nations, mahouts and their elephants are forced to work illegal timber cutting. No safety rules are required in illegal logging, so those jobs are dangerous, and accidents are far too common.

SAVE THE ELEPHANT!

Scientists believe that the loss of elephants in Africa and Asia will change the landscape in dramatic—and possibly negative—ways. Many nations with wild elephant populations have established preserves and refuges for elephant populations. Unfortunately, elephants need a great deal of space and do not like to stay within park borders. Preventing poaching on parkland is difficult, and stopping the slaughter outside parks is nearly impossible. **Conservation** agencies, such as the World Wildlife Fund and the African Wildlife Foundation, work with governments to safeguard land for elephants and train and equip park rangers. These agencies also study the results of elephants and humans living close together.

An Asian elephant pulls a log out of a forest in India.

*A volunteer feeds an orphaned African elephant before
it is flown to a wildlife center in Kenya.*

Because of their size, elephants play an important role in the natural habitats in which they live. Most people recognize that elephants have value, but they do not want elephants to interfere with human needs. It is understandable that farmers do not want elephants to destroy their crops. That situation can be controlled. It is difficult to understand killing an elephant in order to make chopsticks or dice from the animal's tusks. The message is clear, and humans must listen to it: save the elephants!

Glossary

conservation (kon-sur-VAY-shun) act of protecting wilderness and wildlife

forage (FOR-ej) the act of seeking for, or the food itself found in the wild

herbivores (HUR-buh-vors) animals that eat only plants

incisors (in-SY-zurz) any front teeth designed specifically for cutting or gnawing

ivory (EYE-vur-ee) the material elephant tusks are made of

juvenile (JOO-vuh-nile) the young of an animal group

keystone species (KEE-stohn SPEE-sheez) a species that other plants and animals depend on for survival

mahouts (muh-HOWTS) keepers or drivers of working elephants

matriarch (MAY-tree-ark) the female head of a family, tribe, or herd

migrating (MY-grayt-ing) moving from one country, region, or place to another

Moeritherium (meer-ih-THEER-ee-um) an early elephant species that lived on earth 45 to 55 million years ago

musth (MUHST) the state or condition of sexual readiness in male elephants

predators (PREH-duh-turz) animals that hunt and kill other animals for food

puberty (PYOO-ber-tee) a period or age at which a person or animal becomes capable of producing young

subspecies (SUB-spee-sheez) a further division of the animals within a species

For More Information

Watch It

Corwin's Quest—The Elephant's Trunk, DVD (Silver Spring, MD: Discovery Communications, 2007)

Elephants and Lions, DVD (Los Angeles: Delta Entertainment, 2002)

Nature: Echo of the Elephants, DVD (Chicago: Questar Inc., 2005)

Read It

Barnes, Julia. *Elephants at Work*. Milwaukee, WI: Gareth Stevens Publishing, 2005.

Darling, Kathy. *Elephant Hospital*. Brookfield, CT: Millbrook Press, 2000.

Morgan, Jody. *Elephant Rescue: Changing the Future for Endangered Wildlife*. Richmond Hill, Ontario: Firefly Books, 2004.

Redmond, Ian. *Eyewitness*: *Elephant*. New York: DK Children, 2000.

Ring, Susan. *Project Elephant*. Calgary, Alberta: Weigl Educational Publishers Ltd, 2003.

Turner, Matt. *Animals Under Threat: Asian Elephant*. Chicago, Heinemann, 2005.

Look It Up

Visit our Web page for lots of links about elephants:
http://www.childsworld.com/links

Note to Parents, Teachers, and Librarians: We routinely verify our Web links to make sure they are safe, active sites—so encourage your readers to check them out!

The Animal Kingdom
Where Do Elephants Fit In?

Kingdom: Animalia

Phylum: Chordata
(animals with backbones)

Class: Mammalia

Order: Proboscidea

Family: Elephantidae

Genus: *Elephas, Loxodonta*

Species:
Loxodonta africana
(African savanna elephant)

Loxodonta cyclotis
(African forest elephant)

Elephas maximus (Asian elephant)

Subspecies:
Elephas maximus indicus
(Indian elephant)

Elephas maximus maximus
(Sri Lankan elephant)

Elephas maximus sumatrensis
(Sumatran elephant)

Elephas maximus borneensis
(Borneo elephant)

Index

African elephants, 6, *7*, 8, *9*, 11, *15*, 18, *19*, 22, *22*, 25–26, *26*, 31–32, *32, 36*
Andouma water hole, 8
Asian elephants, 12, *12*, 16, 18, *21*, 24, *25*, 27–28, *29*, 33–34, *35*

babies. *See* calves.
bachelor herds, 23
Borneo elephants, 24, 28
bulls, 8, 10, 15, 16, 20, 23, 27
bush elephants. *See* savanna elephants.

calves, 8, 11, 14, *15*, 20, 22–23, 28, *36*
colors, 26, 27, 28
communication, 20, *29*
cows, 6, 8, 10, 15, 16, 20, 22, 23, 26, 27

deaths, 10, 18, 33
dirt baths, 8, *12*, 13
discipline, 23
dugongs, 28
dung, *19*, 20

ears, 11, 13, 25, 26, 27
endangered species, 33

farming, 16, 33, 37
females. *See* cows.
fighting. *See* sparring.
food, 6, 16, 18–19, 22, 24–25, 28
forest elephants, 6, 8, 10, *10*, 18, 26

fossils, 31

habitats, 6, *7*, 25–26, 27, 32, 33, 37
height, 8, 11, 22
Hensman, Rory, 37
herbivores, 6
herds, 8, *9*, 10, 20, 23, 25, 26, 31–32, 33
humans, 9, 10, 11, 15, 16, 32, *32*, 33, 37
hyraxes, 30

Indian elephants, 24, 27
intelligence, 16, 18
ivory, 9–10, *10*, 15, 33, 37

juveniles, 22–23, *22*

keystone species, 18

Laos, 24, *25*
life span, 11

mahouts (trainers), 24, 34
males. *See* bulls.
manatees, 28, *30*
mastodons, 31
mating, 20
matriarchs, 6, 8, 20, 22, 23
memory, 16, 18
migration, 8, 20, 25, 33
Moeritherium, 31
mourning, 18
musth, 23

nursing, 22

orphans, 23

poaching, 9, 15, 32, 37
population, 6, 26, 28, 31–32, 33
predators, 14
pregnancy, 20
pygmy elephants. *See* forest elephants.

salt, 20, *21*
savanna elephants, 8, 16, 18, 24, 25–26
senses, 25, 27, 37
skin, 11, 13, 14, 27
social patterns, 20
sparring, *22*, 23
Sri Lankan elephants, 24, 27–28
Sumatran elephants, 24, 27
superherds, 20

tails, 18, 28
timber industry, 33–34, *35*
tools, 18, *19*
trunks, 6, 8, 11–13, *12*, 14, 18, 27, 31
tusks, 8, 9, *10*, 11, 14–15, *15*, 25, 26, 27, 31, 37

walking, 13, 22
water, 6, 8, 11, 13, *17*, 18, 24, 25, 33
weight, 8, 10, 11, 20, 22, 26, 27

Zakouma National Park, 6, *9*, 10, 20

About the Author

Sophie Lockwood is a former teacher and a longtime writer. She writes textbooks, newspaper articles, and magazine articles. Sophie enjoys writing about animals and their habits. The most interesting part of her research, Sophie says, is learning how scientists apply their knowledge to save endangered species. She lives with her husband in the foothills of the Blue Ridge Mountains.

This Book Belongs
to
Mrs. Klozik